TOP HITS OF 2018

ISBN: 978-1-5400-3595-0

Visit Hal Leonard Online at
www.halleonard.com

Contact Us:
Hal Leonard
7777 West Bluemound Road
Milwaukee, WI 53213
Email: info@halleonard.com

In Europe contact:
Hal Leonard Europe Limited
Distribution Centre, Newmarket Road
Bury St Edmunds, Suffolk, IP33 3YB
Email: info@halleonardeurope.com

In Australia contact:
Hal Leonard Australia Pty. Ltd.
4 Lentara Court
Cheltenham, Victoria, 3192 Australia
Email: info@halleonard.com.au

Call Out My Name

Words and Music by Abel Tesfaye, Adam Feeney and Nicolas Jaar

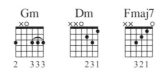

*Capo I

Strum Pattern: 8
Pick Pattern: 8

Intro
Very slow, in 2

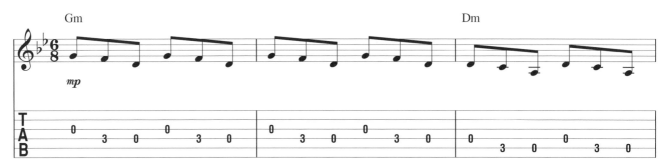

*Optional: To match recording, place capo at 1st fret.

Verse

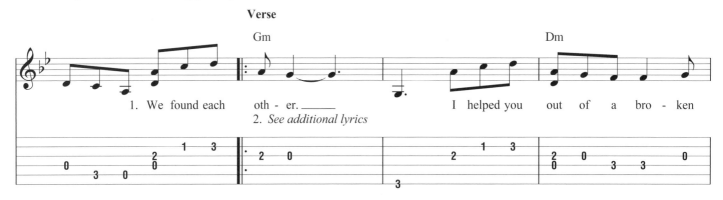

1. We found each oth - er. _____
2. *See additional lyrics*

I helped you out of a bro - ken

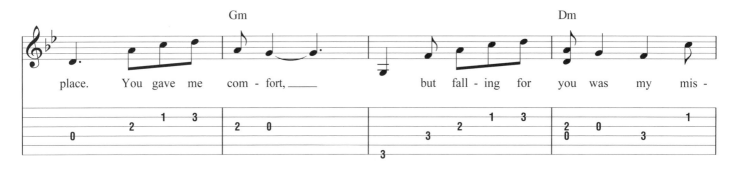

place. You gave me com - fort, _____ but fall - ing for you was my mis -

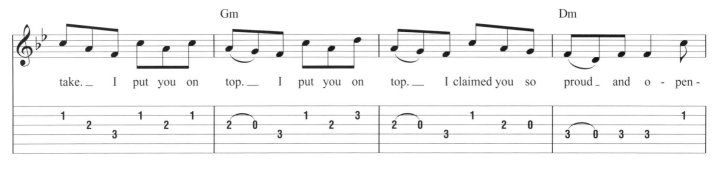

take. _ I put you on top. _ I put you on top. _ I claimed you so proud _ and o - pen -

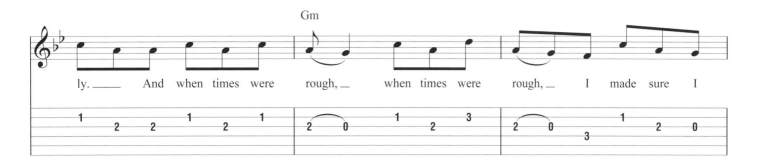

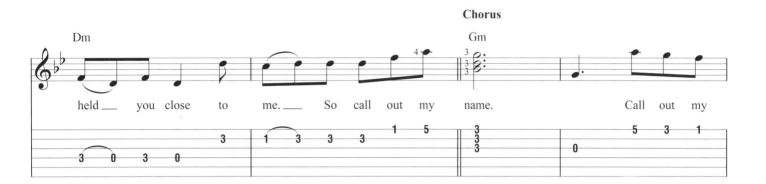

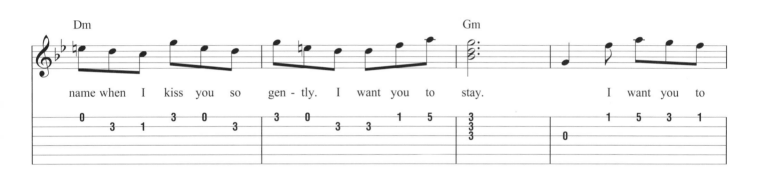

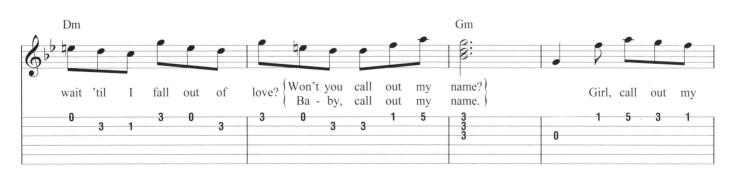

Outro

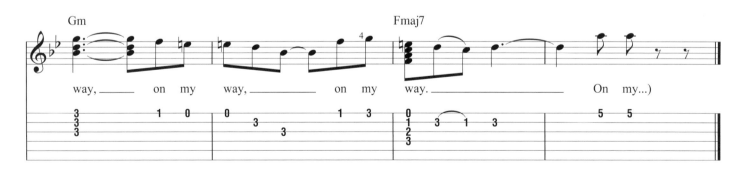

Additional Lyrics

2. I said I didn't feel nothing, baby, but I lied.
   I almost cut a piece of myself for your life.
   Guess I was just another pitstop 'til you made up your mind.
   You just wasted my time.
   You're on top. I put you on top.
   I claimed you so proud and openly, babe.
   And when times were rough, when times were rough,
   I made sure I held you close to me.

Meant to Be

Words and Music by Bleta Rexha, Josh Miller, Tyler Hubbard and David Garcia

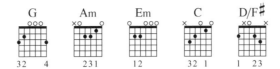

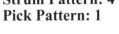

*Capo III

Strum Pattern: 4
Pick Pattern: 1

Intro
Moderately slow, in 2

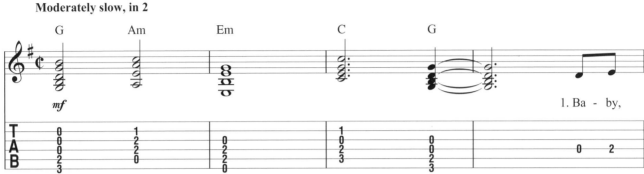

1. Ba - by,

*Optional: To match recording, place capo at 3rd fret.

Verse

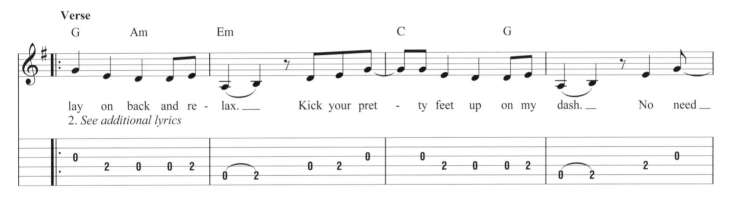

lay on back and re - lax. ___ Kick your pret - ty feet up on my dash. ___ No need ___
2. *See additional lyrics*

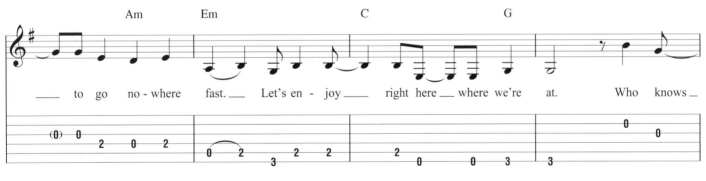

___ to go no - where fast. Let's en - joy ___ right here ___ where we're at. Who knows ___

___ where this road is sup - posed to lead? ___ We got noth - in' but time. ___ As long ___

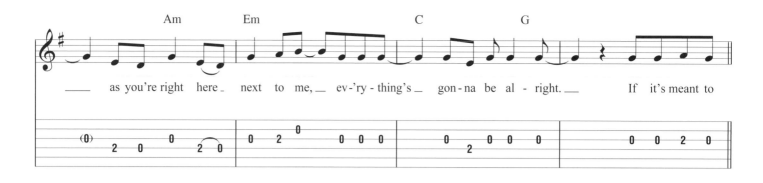

as you're right here _ next to me, _ ev-'ry-thing's _ gon-na be al-right. _ If it's meant to

℠ Chorus

be, it-'ll be, _____ it-'ll be. _ Ba-by, just let it be. _____ If it's meant to

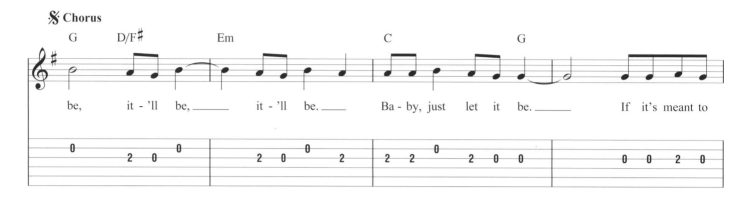

be, it-'ll be, _____ it-'ll be. _ Ba-by, just let it be. _____ So, won't you

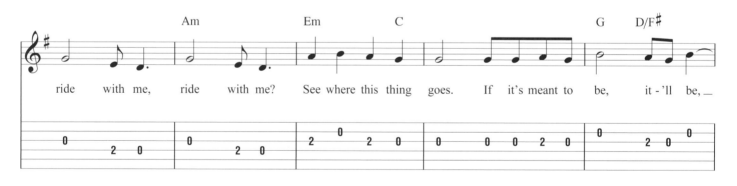

ride with me, ride with me? See where this thing goes. If it's meant to be, it-'ll be,

To Coda ⊕

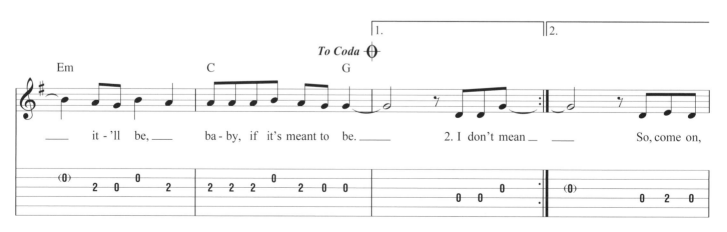

_ it-'ll be, _ ba-by, if it's meant to be. _ 2. I don't mean _ _ So, come on,

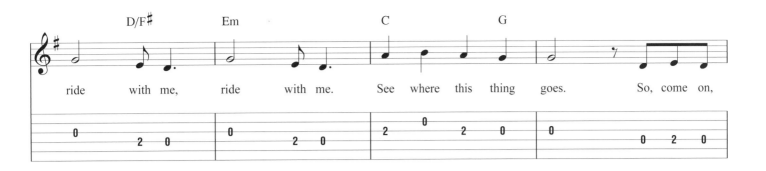

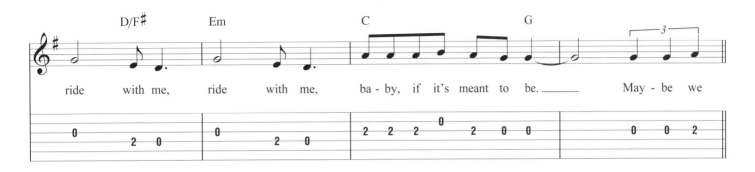

Bridge

D.S. al Coda

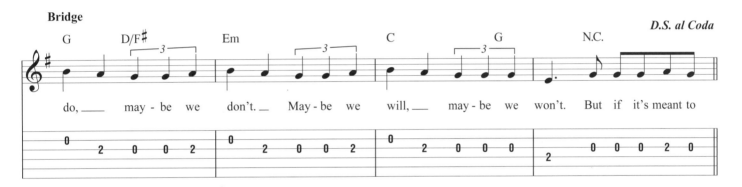

✛ **Coda**

Outro

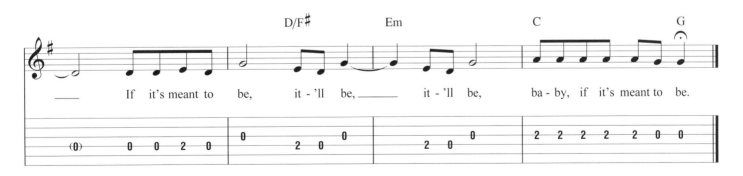

Additional Lyrics

2. I don't mean to be so uptight, but my heart's been hurt a couple times
   By a couple guys that didn't treat me right. I ain't gonna lie, I ain't gonna lie,
   'Cause I'm tired of the fake love. Show me what you're made of. Boy, make me believe.
   Whoa, hold up, girl. Don't you know you're beautiful? And it's easy to see.

Delicate

Words and Music by Taylor Swift, Max Martin and Shellback

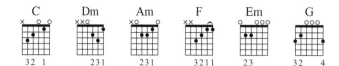

Strum Pattern: 3
Pick Pattern: 3

Intro
Moderately slow

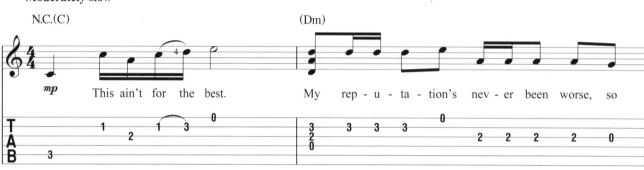

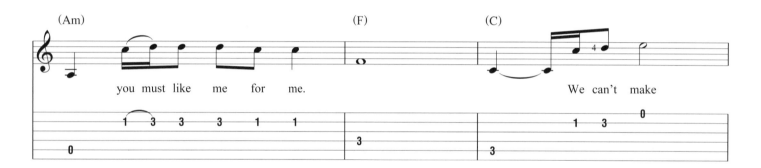

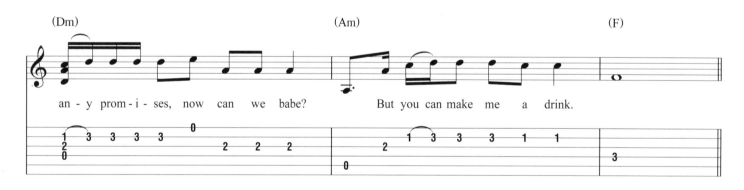

Verse

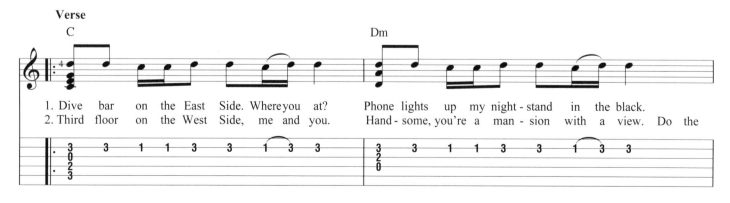

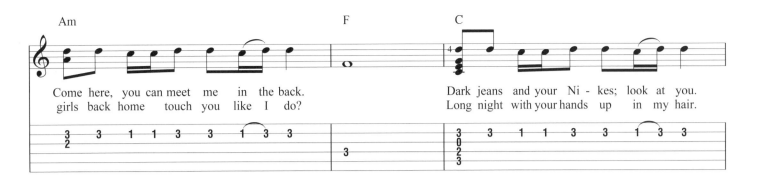

Come here, you can meet me in the back.
girls back home touch you like I do?

Dark jeans and your Ni - kes; look at you.
Long night with your hands up in my hair.

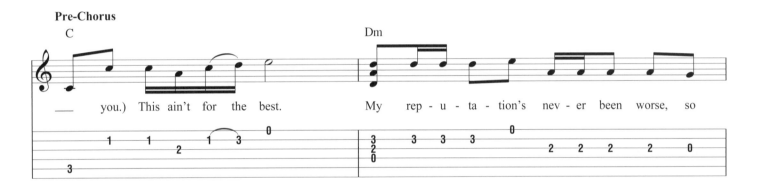

Oh damn, nev - er seen that col - or blue.
Ech - oes of your foot - steps on the stairs.

Just think of the fun things we could do.
Stay here, hon - ey, I don't want to share.

('Cause I like

Pre-Chorus

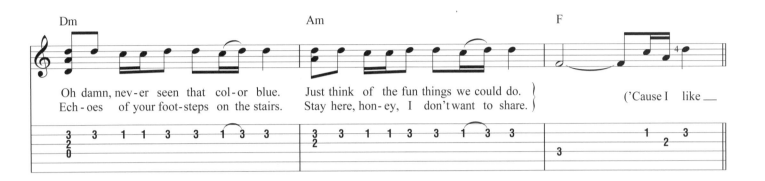

you.) This ain't for the best.

My rep - u - ta - tion's nev - er been worse, so

you must like me for me.

(Yeah, I want you.) We can't make

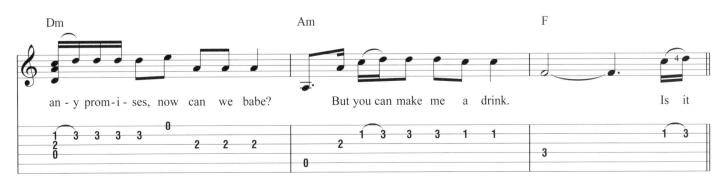

an - y prom - i - ses, now can we babe?

But you can make me a drink.

Is it

Chorus

cool that I said all that? Is it chill that you're in my head? 'Cause I know that it's del - i - cate.

(Del - i - cate.) Is it cool that I said all that? Is it too soon to do this yet? 'Cause I

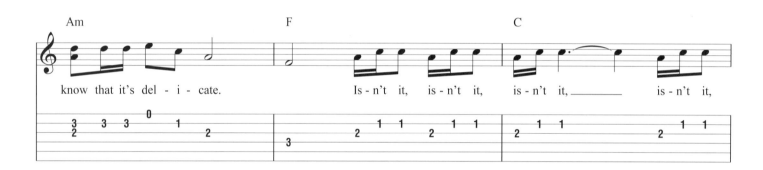

know that it's del - i - cate. Is - n't it, is - n't it, is - n't it, _____ is - n't it,

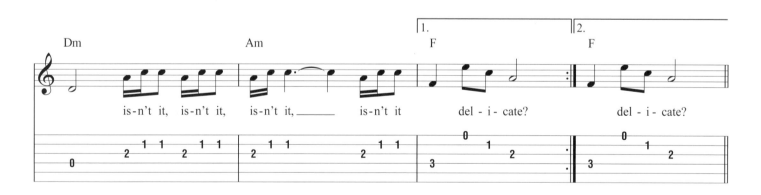

is - n't it, is - n't it, is - n't it, _____ is - n't it del - i - cate? del - i - cate?

Bridge

Some - times, I won - der _____ when you sleep, _____ are you ev - er dream -

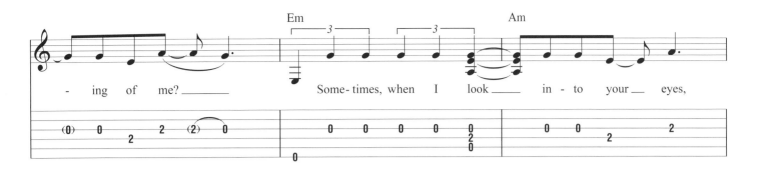

-ing of me? _____ Some-times, when I look _____ in - to your ___ eyes,

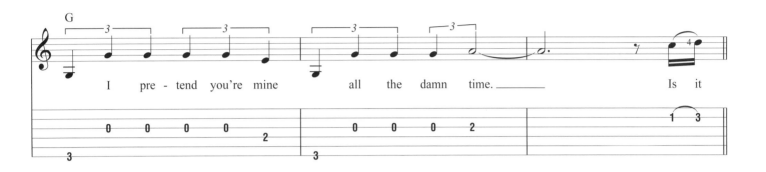

I pre - tend you're mine all the damn time. _____ Is it

Chorus

cool that I said all that? Is it chill that you're in my head? 'Cause I know that it's del - i - cate.

(Del - i - cate.) Is it cool that I said all that? Is it too soon to do this yet? 'Cause I

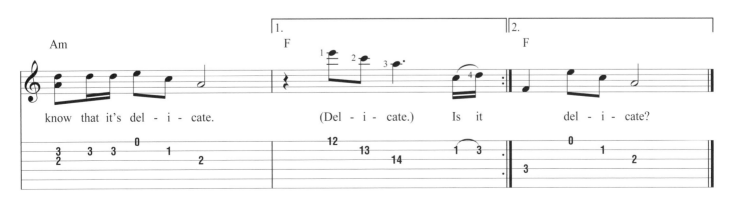

know that it's del - i - cate. (Del - i - cate.) Is it del - i - cate?

Girls Like You

Words and Music by Adam Levine, Brittany Hazzard, Jason Evigan and Henry Walter

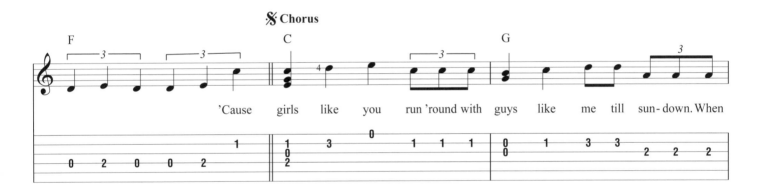

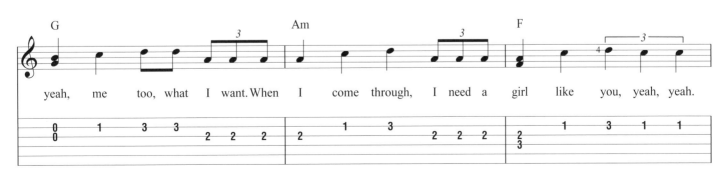

3rd time, To Coda

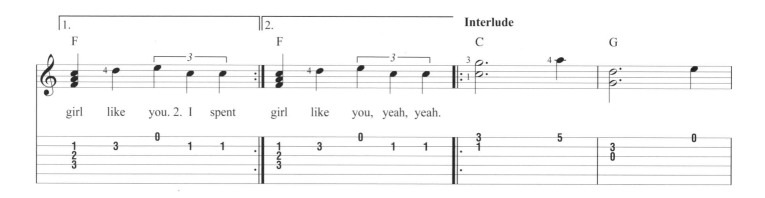

last time, ___ yeah. May-be I know that I'm drunk. May-be I know you're the one.

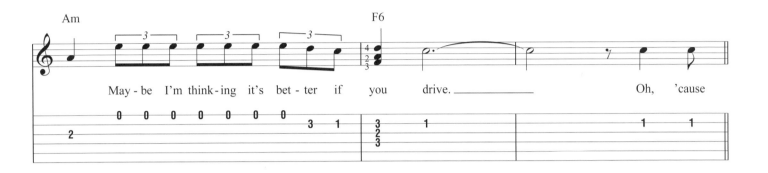

May-be I'm think-ing it's bet-ter if you drive. ___ Oh, 'cause

Chorus

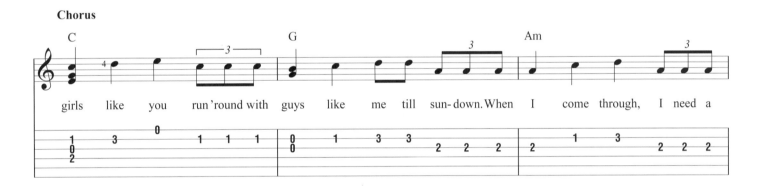

girls like you run 'round with guys like me till sun-down. When I come through, I need a

D.S. al Coda ⊕ **Coda** **Outro**

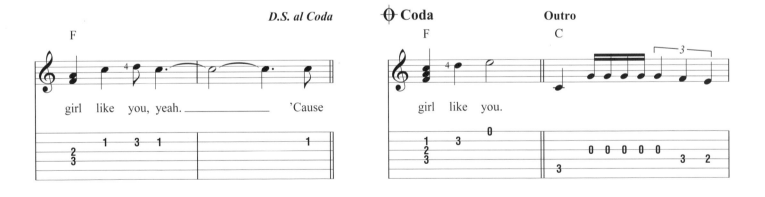

girl like you, yeah. ___ 'Cause girl like you.

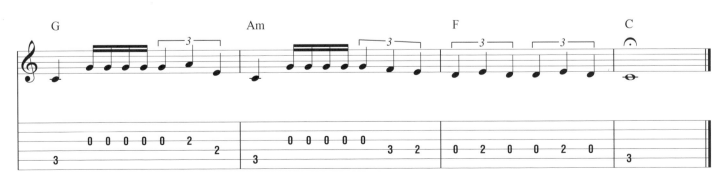

In My Blood

Words and Music by Shawn Mendes, Geoff Warburton, Teddy Geiger and Scott Harris

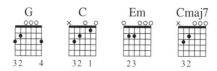

*Tune down 1 step:
(low to high) D-G-C-F-A-D

Strum Pattern: 3
Pick Pattern: 3

Intro
Slow

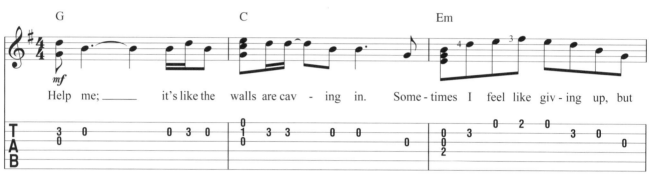

Help me; _____ it's like the walls are cav - ing in. Some - times I feel like giv - ing up, but

*Optional: To match recording, tune down 1 step.

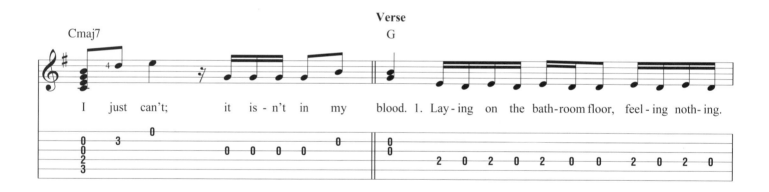

I just can't; it is - n't in my blood. 1. Lay - ing on the bath-room floor, feel - ing noth- ing.

I'm o - ver whelmed and in - se - cure; give me some-thing I could take to ease my mind slow - ly.

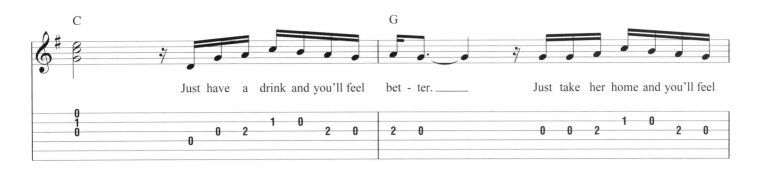

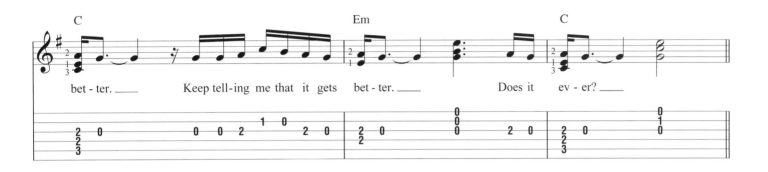

𝄋 Pre-Chorus

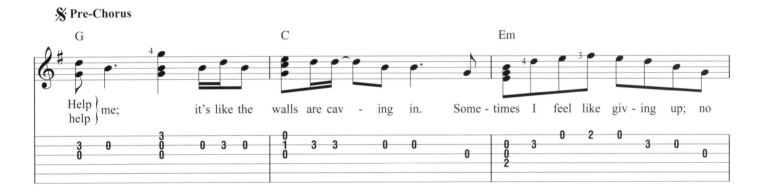

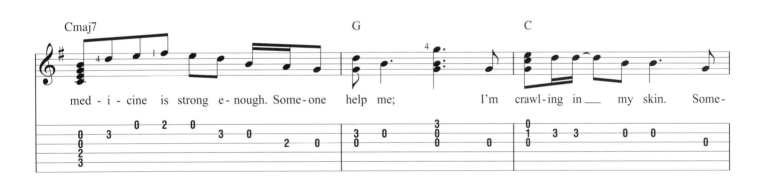

Chorus

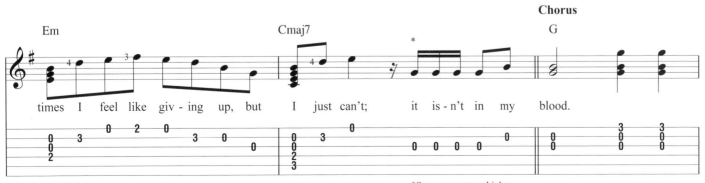

*Sung one octave higher.

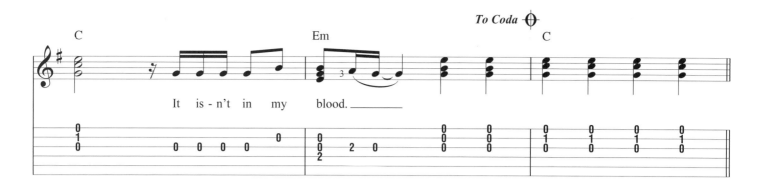

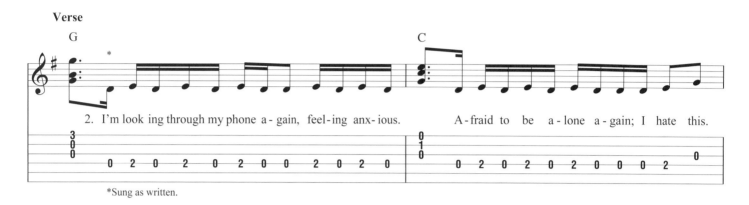

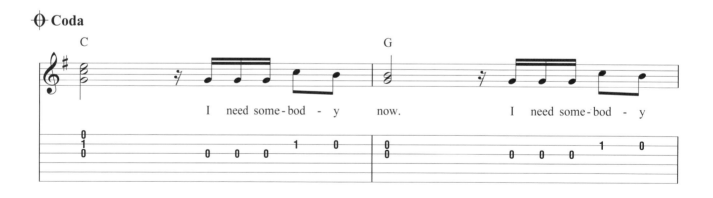

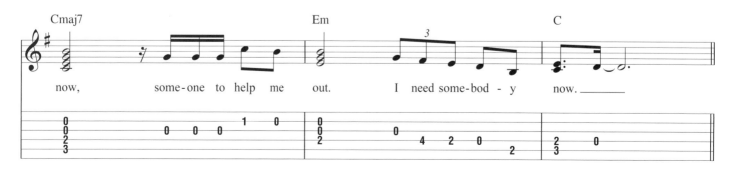

18

Pre-Chorus

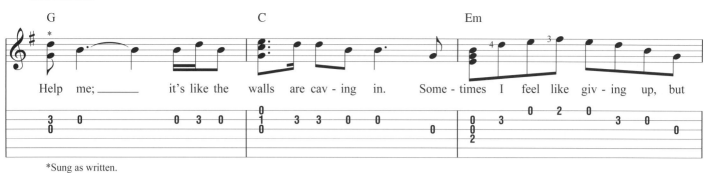

Help me;_____ it's like the walls are cav - ing in. Some - times I feel like giv - ing up, but

*Sung as written.

Outro-Chorus

I just can't; it is - n't in my blood. It is - n't in my

**Sung one octave higher till end.

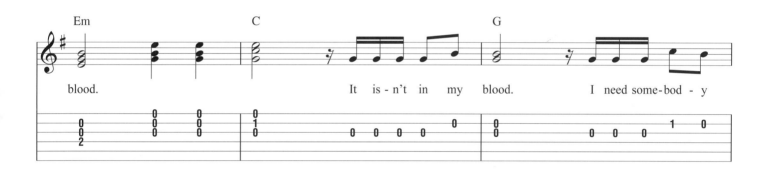

blood. It is - n't in my blood. I need some - bod - y

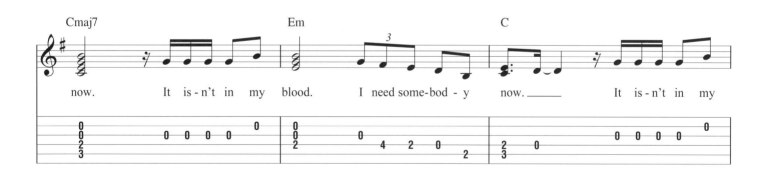

now. It is - n't in my blood. I need some - bod - y now._____ It is - n't in my

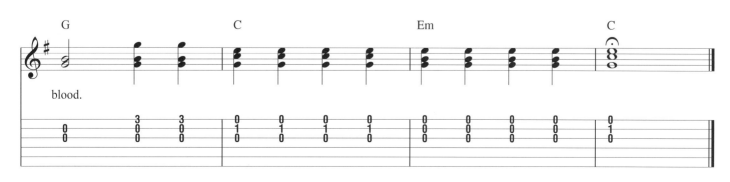

blood.

The Middle

Words and Music by Sarah Aarons, Marcus Lomax, Jordan Johnson,
Anton Zaslavski, Kyle Trewartha, Michael Trewartha and Stefan Johnson

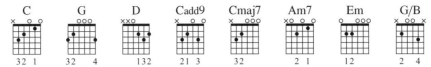

Strum Pattern: 1
Pick Pattern: 5

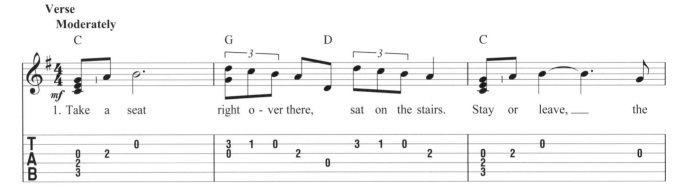

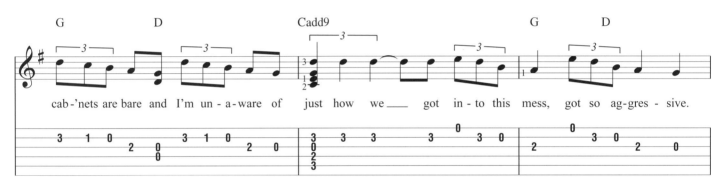

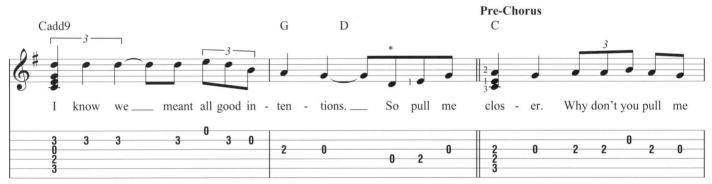

*Sung one octave higher.

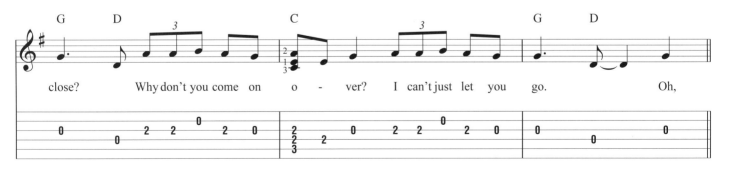

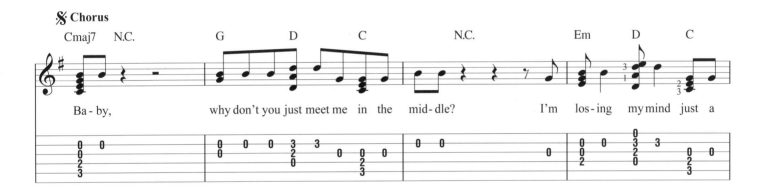

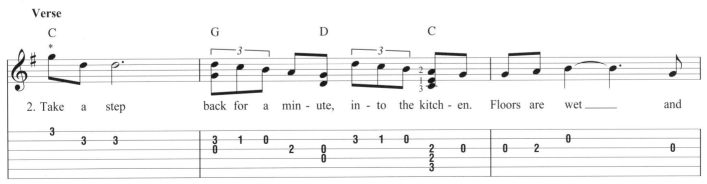

*Sung as written.

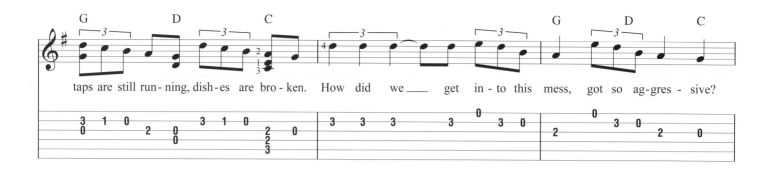

taps are still run-ning, dish-es are bro-ken. How did we __ get in-to this mess, got so ag-gres-sive?

Pre-Chorus

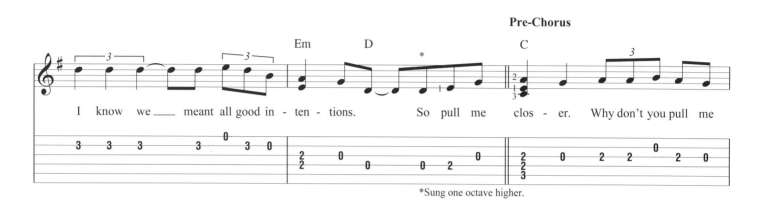

I know we __ meant all good in - ten - tions. So pull me clos - er. Why don't you pull me

*Sung one octave higher.

D.S. al Coda

close? Why don't you come on o - ver? I can't just let you go. __ Oh.

⊕ Coda

Bridge

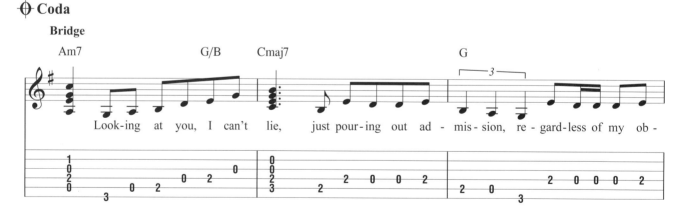

Look-ing at you, I can't lie, just pour-ing out ad - mis-sion, re-gard-less of my ob-

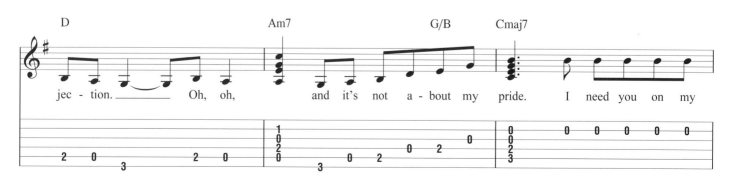

jec - tion. __ Oh, oh, and it's not a - bout my pride. I need you on my

Chorus

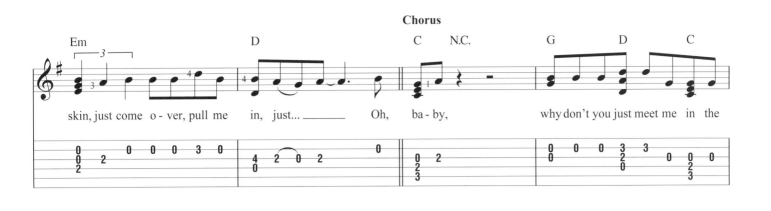

Outro-Chorus

2nd time, w/ voc. ad lib.

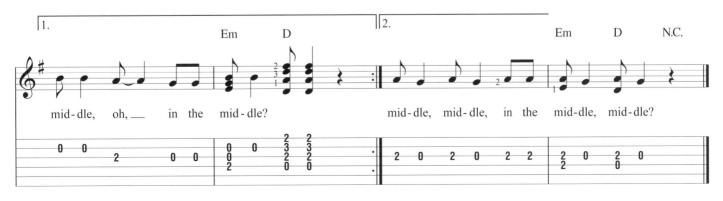

A Million Dreams

from THE GREATEST SHOWMAN
Words and Music by Benj Pasek and Justin Paul

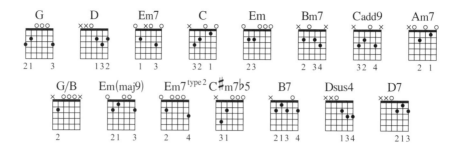

Strum Pattern: 6
Pick Pattern: 4

Intro
Moderately slow, in 2

Verse

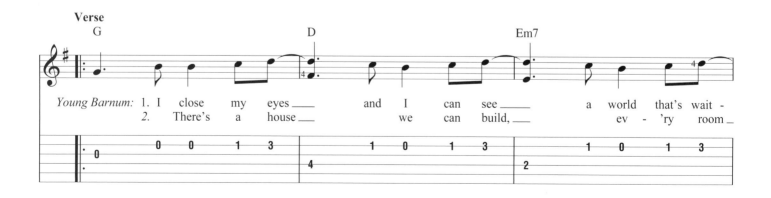

Young Barnum: 1. I close my eyes ___ and I can see ___ a world that's wait-
2. There's a house ___ we can build, ___ ev-'ry room ___

Copyright © 2017 Breathelike Music, Pick In A Pinch Music and T C F Music Publishing, Inc.
All Rights for Breathelike Music and Pick In A Pinch Music Administered Worldwide by Kobalt Songs Music Publishing
All Rights Reserved   Used by Permission

-ing up ___ for me ___ that I call my own.
___ in - side ___ is filled ___ with things from far a - way.

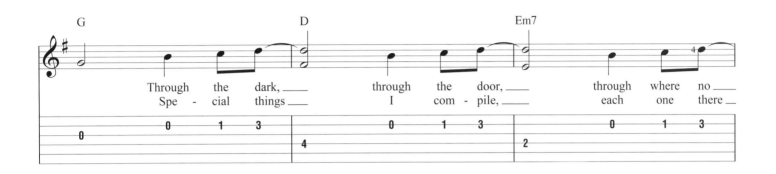

Through the dark, ___ through the door, ___ through where no ___
Spe - cial things ___ I com - pile, ___ through each one there ___

___ one's been be - fore, ___ but it feels like home.
___ to make you smile ___ on a rain - y day.

Pre-Chorus

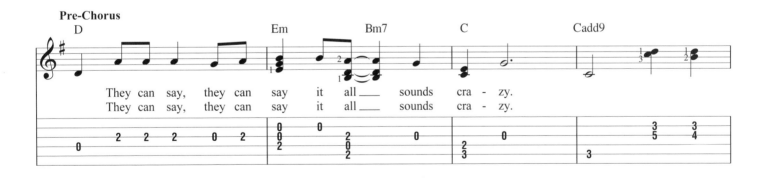

They can say, they can say it all ___ sounds cra - zy.
They can say, they can say it all ___ sounds cra - zy.

They can say, they can say I've lost ___ my mind. ___
They can say, they can say we've lost ___ our minds. ___

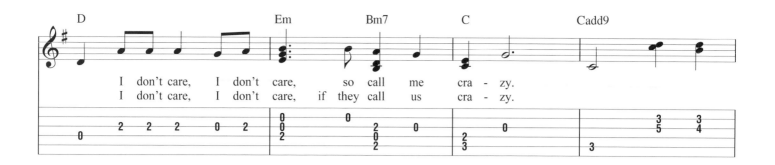

I don't care, I don't care, so call me cra - zy.
I don't care, I don't care, if they call us cra - zy.

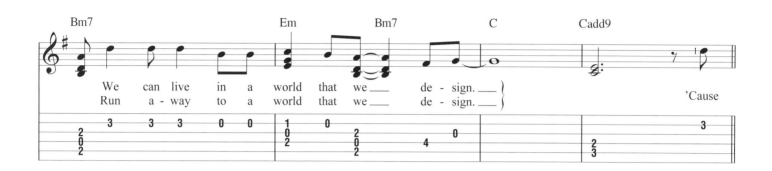

We can live in a world that we _____ de - sign. _____
Run a - way to a world that we _____ de - sign. _____

'Cause

Chorus

ev - 'ry night _____ I lie _____ in bed, the bright - est col - ors fill _____ my head. A

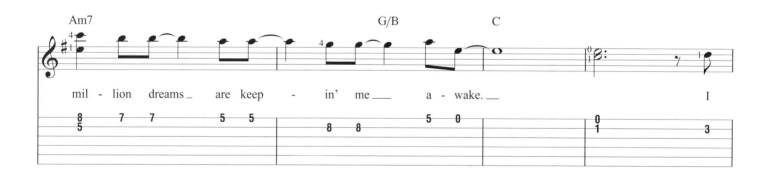

mil - lion dreams _____ are keep - in' me _____ a - wake. _____

I

think of what _____ the world _____ could be, _____ a vi - sion of the one _____ I see. A

mil - lion dreams _ is all ___ it's gon - na take. ___ Oh, a

mil - lion dreams _ for the world we're gon - na make.

1.
Interlude

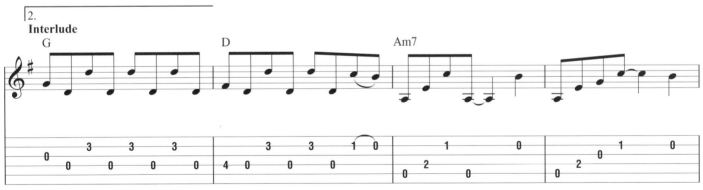

2.
Interlude

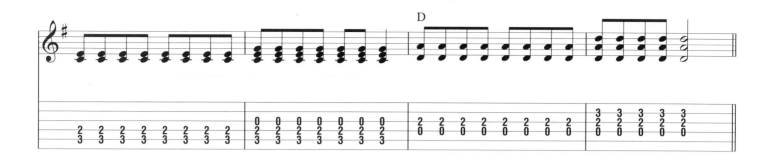

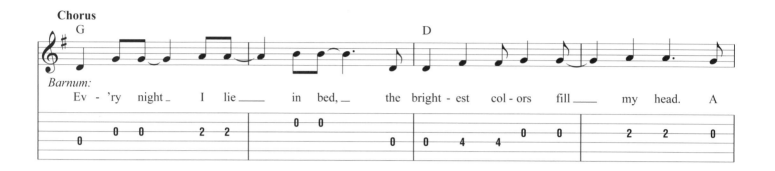

Chorus

Barnum:
Ev - 'ry night I lie in bed, the bright - est col - ors fill my head. A

mil - lion dreams are keep - in' me a - wake. I

think of what the world could be, a vi - sion of the one I see. A

mil - lion dreams is all it's gon - na take. Oh, a

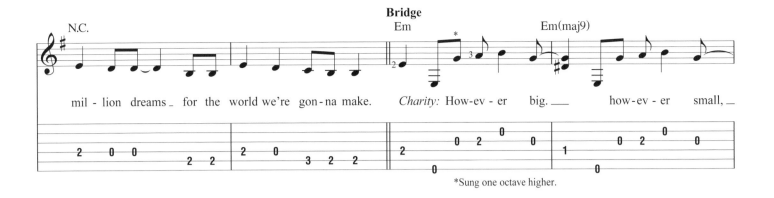

*Sung one octave higher.

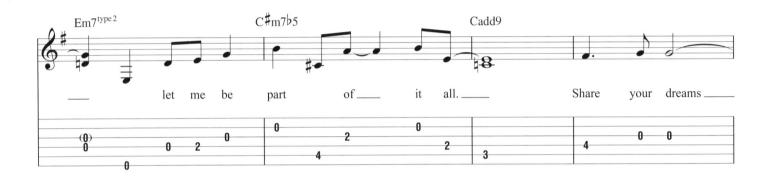

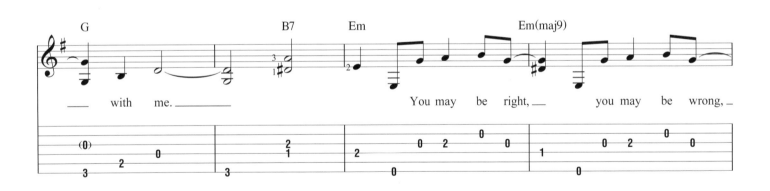

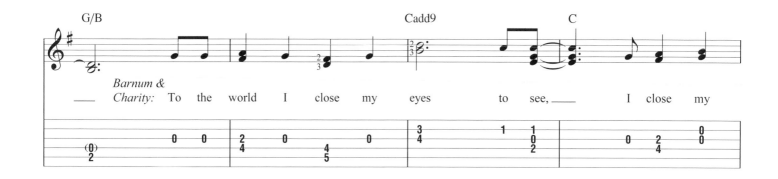

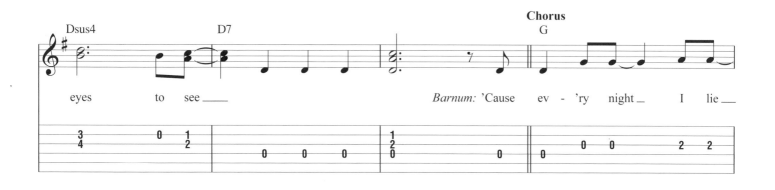

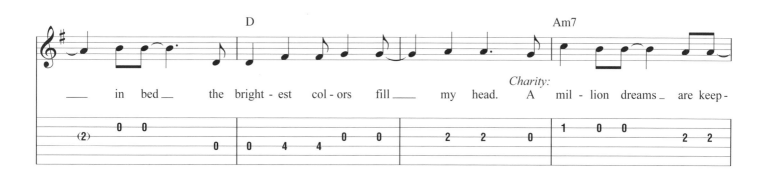

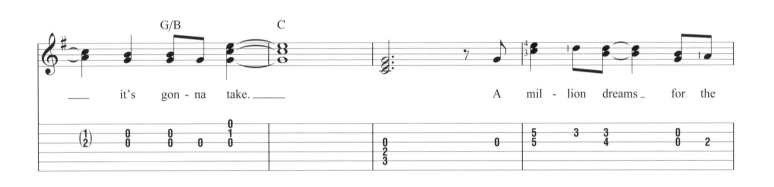

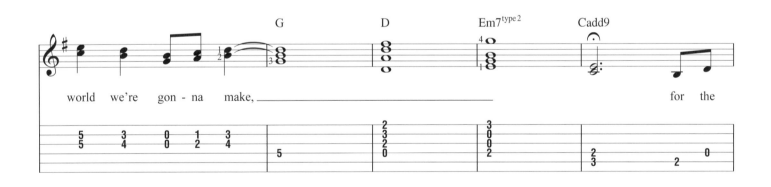

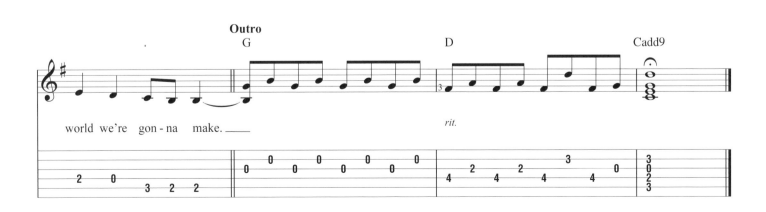

Never Be the Same

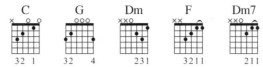

Words and Music by Camila Cabello, Adam Feeney, Noonie Bao,
Leo Rami Dawood, Jacob Ludwig Olofsson and Sasha Yatchenko

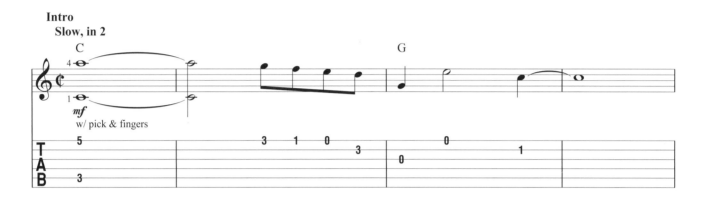

Strum Pattern: 1
Pick Pattern: 1

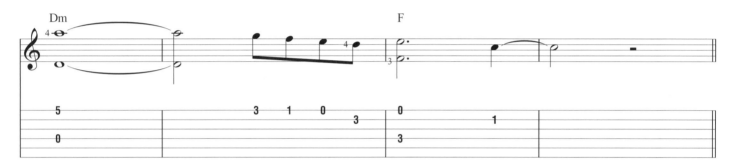

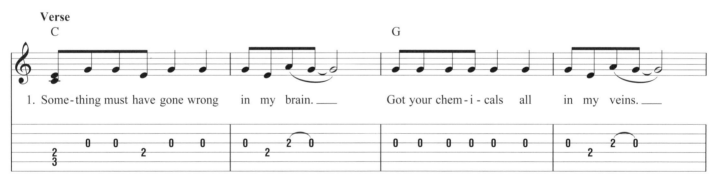

Verse

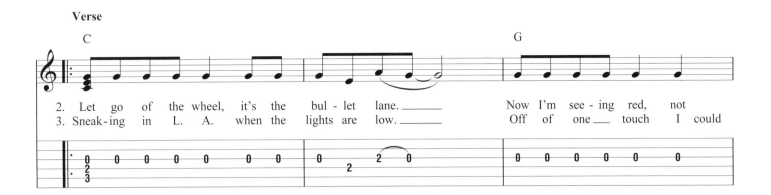

2. Let go of the wheel, it's the bul-let lane. _____ Now I'm see-ing red, not
3. Sneak-ing in L. A. when the lights are low. _____ Off of one ___ touch I could

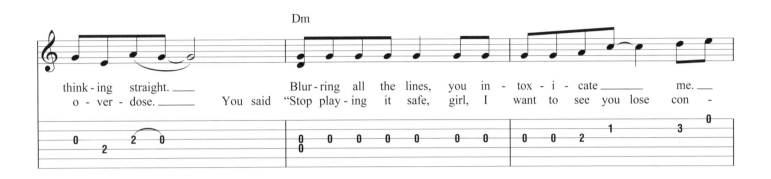

think-ing straight. _____ Blur-ring all the lines, you in-tox-i-cate _____ me. _____
o-ver-dose. _____ You said "Stop play-ing it safe, girl, I want to see you lose con -

Pre-Chorus

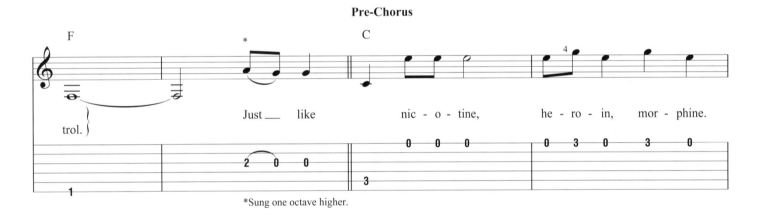

trol. } Just ___ like nic-o-tine, he-ro-in, mor-phine.

*Sung one octave higher.

Sud-den-ly, I'm a fiend ___ and you're all I need. All I need, _____

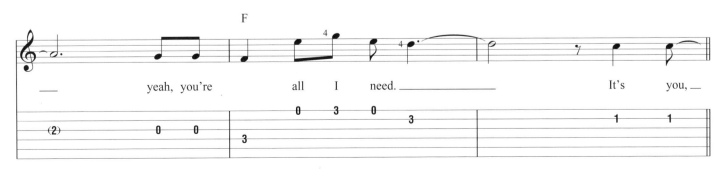

___ yeah, you're all I need. _____ It's you, ___

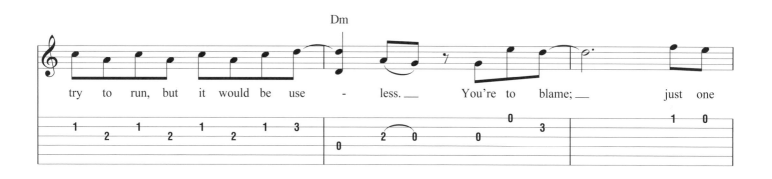

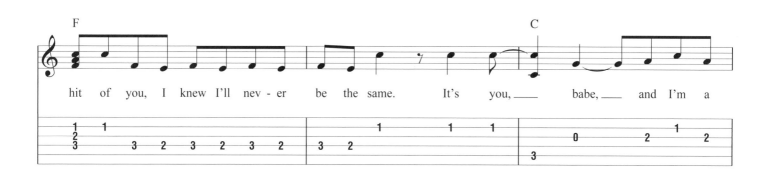

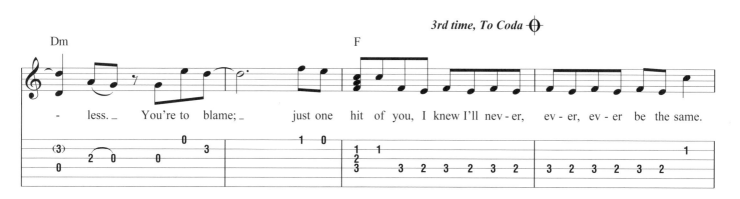

I'll nev-er be the same. _____   I'll nev-er be the same. __

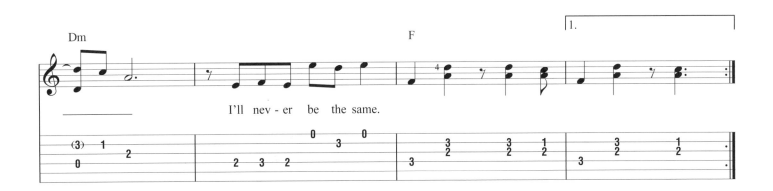

_____   I'll nev-er be the same.

You're _ in my blood, _ you're _ in my veins, _ you're _ in my head. _

*Sung as written.

I   blame. You're _ in my blood, _ you're _ in my veins, _ you're _

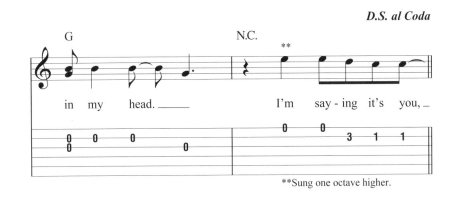

in my head. _____   I'm say-ing it's you, _

**Sung one octave higher.

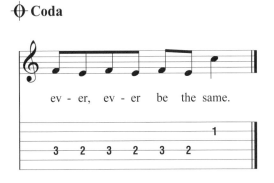

ev - er, ev - er be the same.

No Tears Left to Cry

Words and Music by Ariana Grande, Savan Kotecha, Max Martin and Ilya

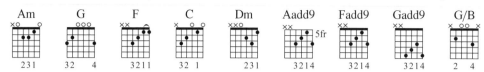

Strum Pattern: 3
Pick Pattern: 3

Chorus
Moderately

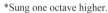

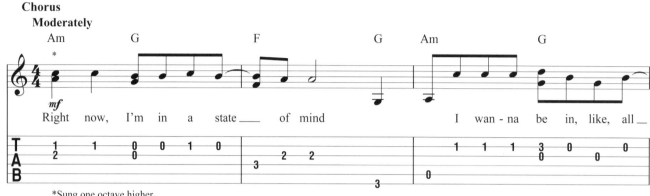

*Sung one octave higher.

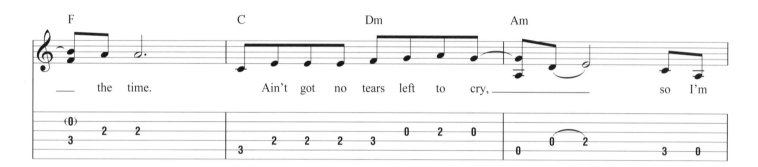

Moderately fast

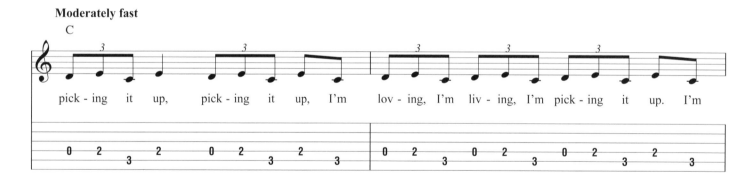

**Lyrics in italics are spoken throughout.

Interlude

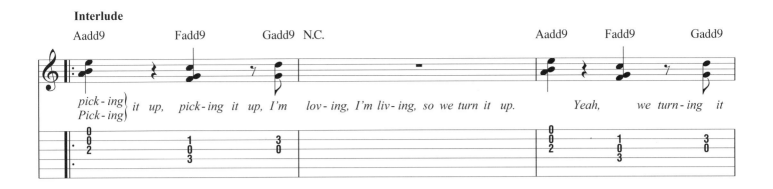

pick-ing } it up, pick-ing it up, I'm lov-ing, I'm liv-ing, so we turn it up. Yeah, we turn-ing it
Pick-ing }

Verse

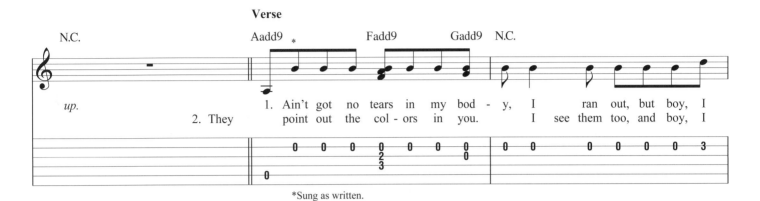

up.

1. Ain't got no tears in my bod - y, I ran out, but boy, I
2. They point out the col - ors in you. I see them too, and boy, I

*Sung as written.

like ___ it, I like ___ it, I like ___ it. ___ Don't mat - ter how, what, where,
like ___ 'em, I like ___ 'em, I like ___ 'em. ___ We're way too fly to par - take

who tries it, } we're out here vib - ing, ___ we vib - ing, we vib - ing. ___
in all this hate, }

Pre-Chorus

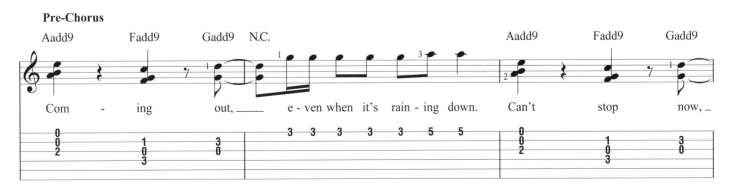

Com - ing out, ___ e - ven when it's rain - ing down. Can't stop now, ___

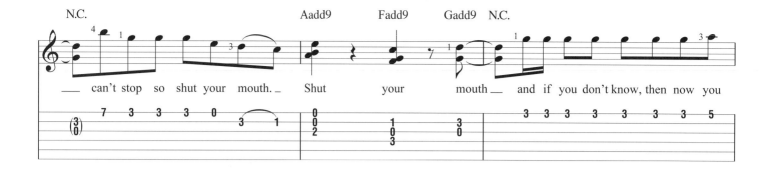

___ can't stop so shut your mouth. ___ Shut your mouth ___ and if you don't know, then now you

Chorus

know it, babe, know it babe, yeah. Right now, I'm in a state ___ of mind ___

*Sung one octave higher, except where noted.

I wan-na be in, like, all ___ the time. ___ Ain't got no tears left to cry, ___

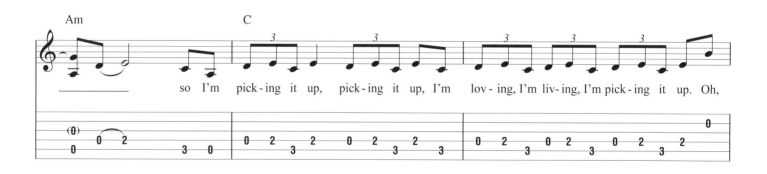

___ so I'm pick-ing it up, pick-ing it up, I'm lov-ing, I'm liv-ing, I'm pick-ing it up. Oh,

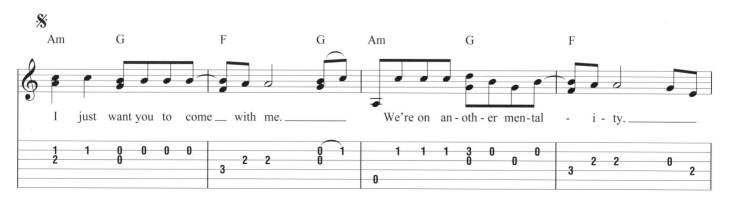

I just want you to come ___ with me. ___ We're on an-oth-er men-tal - i-ty. ___

Ain't got no tears left to cry, _____ so I'm pick-ing it up, pick-ing it up, I'm

3rd time, To Coda ⊕ Chorus

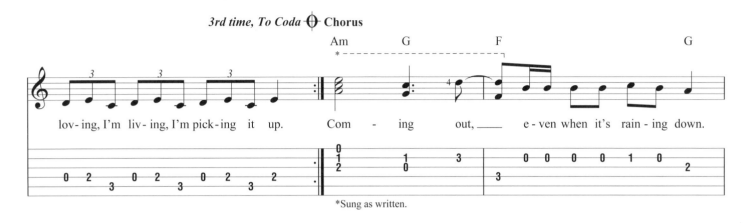

lov-ing, I'm liv-ing, I'm pick-ing it up. Com-ing out, _____ e - ven when it's rain-ing down.

*Sung as written.

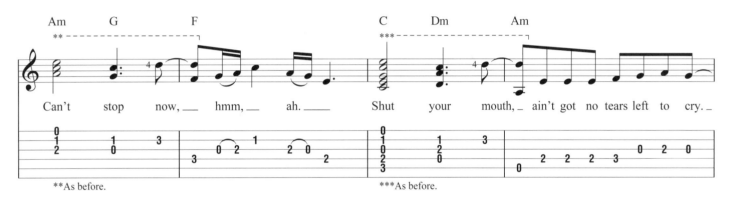

Can't stop now, _ hmm, _ ah. _____ Shut your mouth, _ ain't got no tears left to cry. _

**As before. ***As before.

⊕ **Coda**

D.S. al Coda **Outro**

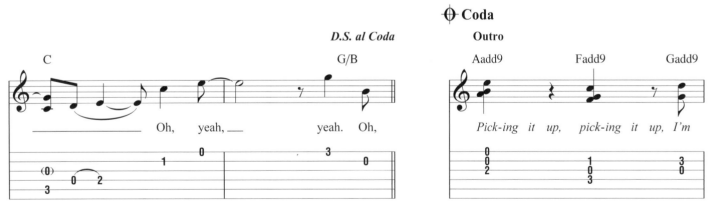

_____ Oh, yeah, _____ yeah. Oh, Pick-ing it up, pick-ing it up, I'm

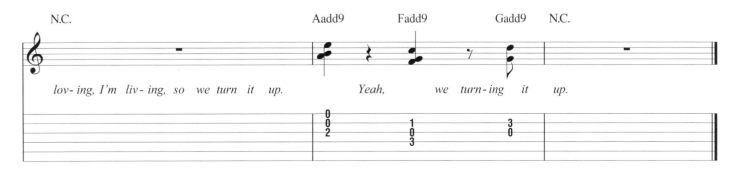

lov-ing, I'm liv-ing, so we turn it up. Yeah, we turn-ing it up.

Say Something

Words and Music by Justin Timberlake, Chris Stapleton, Nate Hills, Larrance Dopson and Timothy Mosley

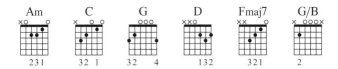

*Capo III

Strum Pattern: 6
Pick Pattern: 5, 6

Intro
Moderately slow

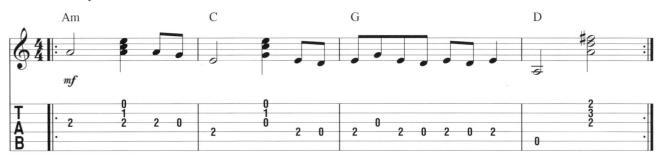

*Optional: To match recording, place capo at 3rd fret.

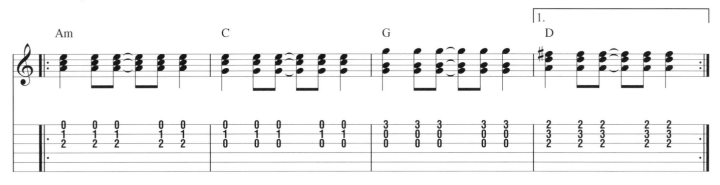

Verse

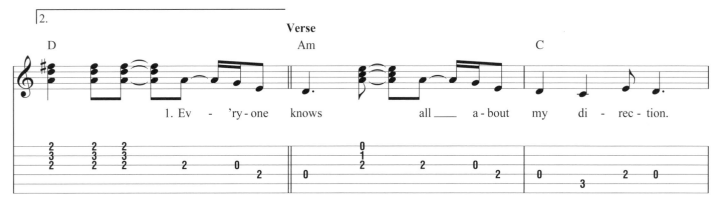

1. Ev - 'ry-one knows all ___ a - bout my di - rec - tion.

And in ___ my heart some - where, ___ I ___ wan - na go ___

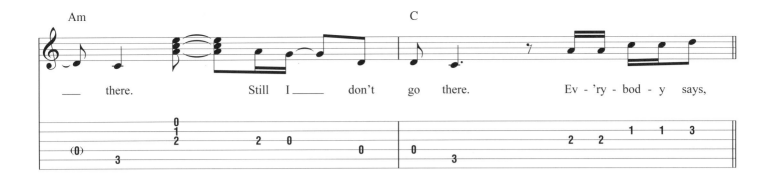

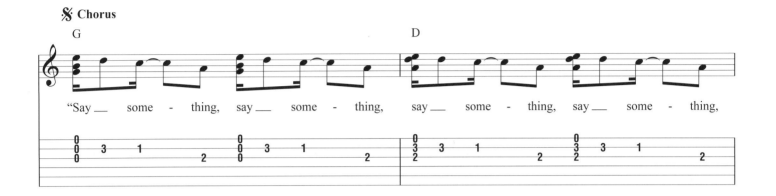

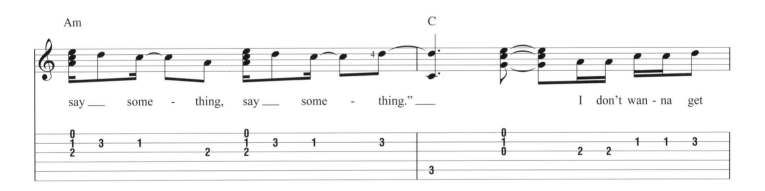

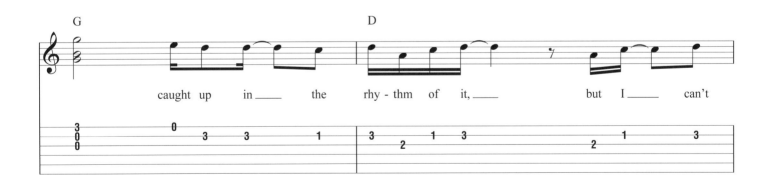

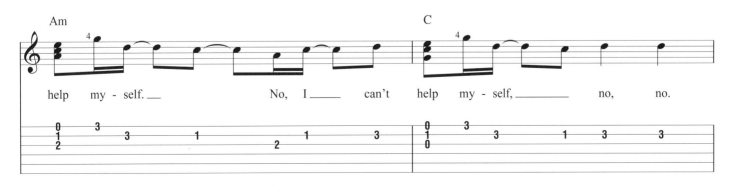

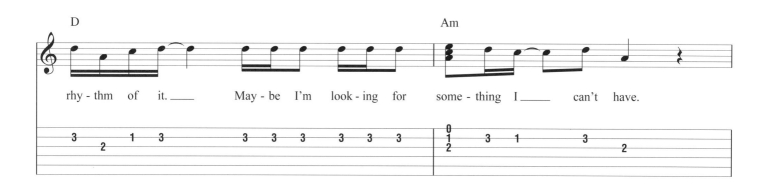

To Coda ⊕

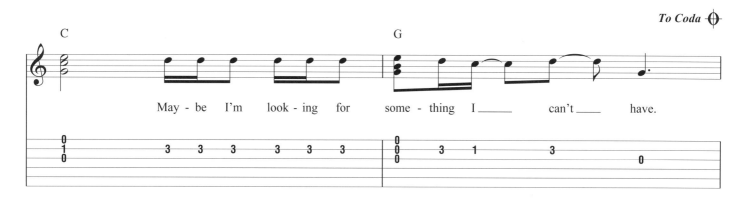

Verse

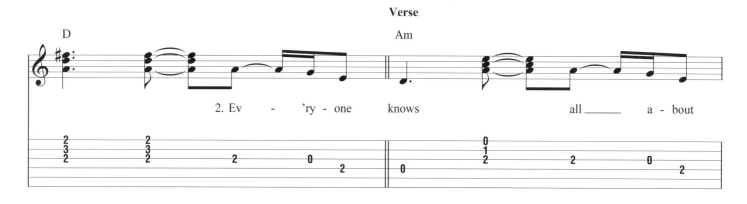

my trans - gres - sions.   Still, in ___ my heart some - where, there's mel - o - dy and

*Chord symbols in parentheses reflect implied harmony.

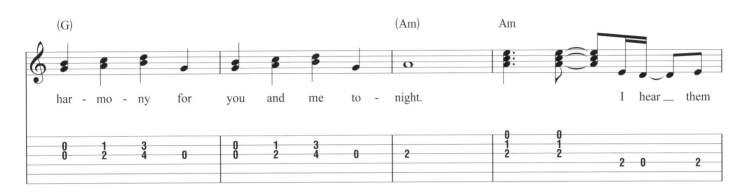

har - mo - ny   for   you   and   me   to - night.   I hear ___ them

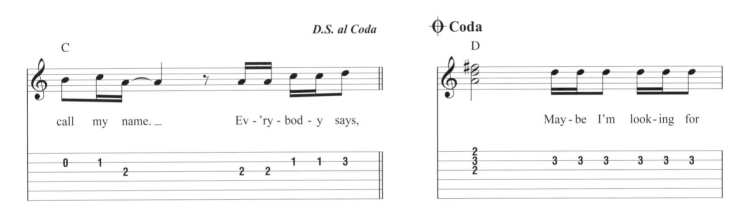

D.S. al Coda   ⊕ **Coda**

call   my   name. ___   Ev - 'ry - bod - y says,   May - be I'm   look - ing for

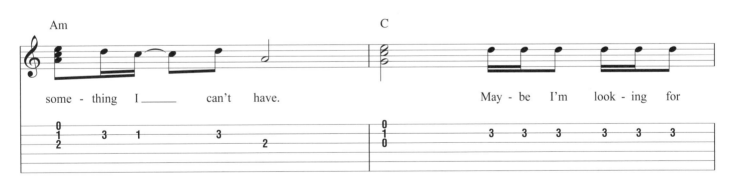

some - thing I ___ can't have.   May - be I'm   look - ing for

Interlude

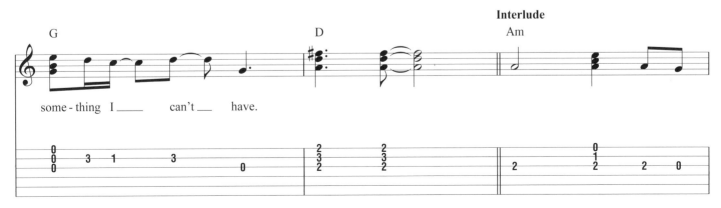

some - thing I ___ can't ___ have.

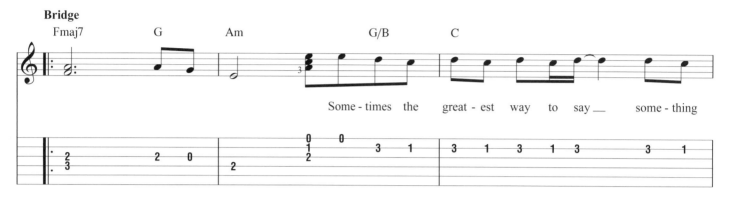

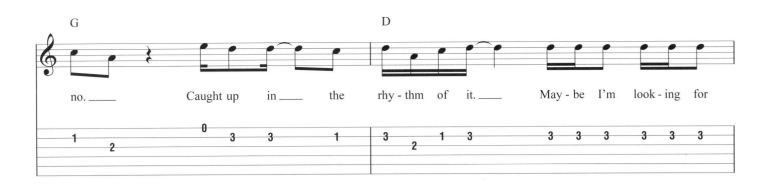

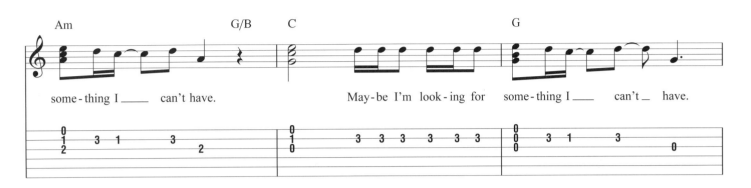

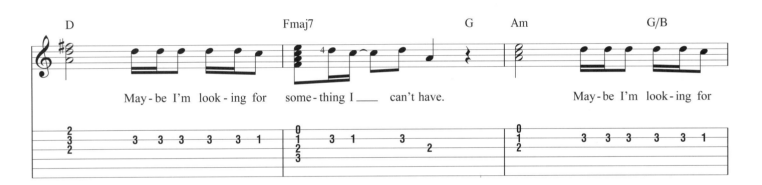

Outro

Whatever It Takes

Words and Music by Dan Reynolds, Wayne Sermon, Ben McKee, Daniel Platzman and Joel Little

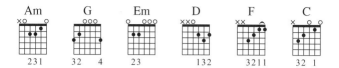

*Capo I

Strum Pattern: 1
Pick Pattern: 5

Intro
Slow, in 2

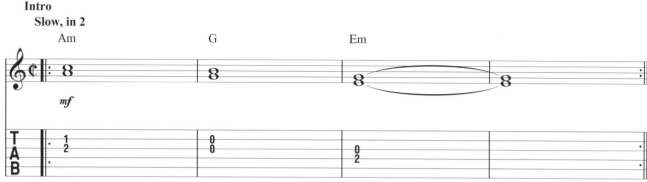

*Optional: To match recording, place capo at 1st fret.

Verse

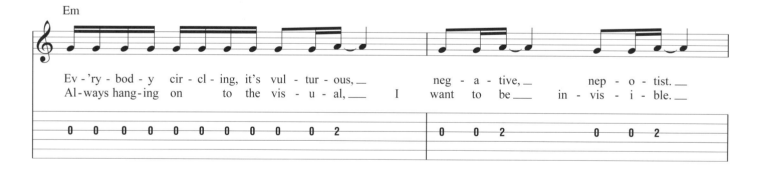

1. Fall-ing too fast to pre-pare for this, ___ trip-ping in the world could be dan-ger-ous. ___
2. Al-ways had a fear of be-ing ty-pi-cal, ___ look-ing at my bod-y, feel-ing mis-'ra-ble. ___

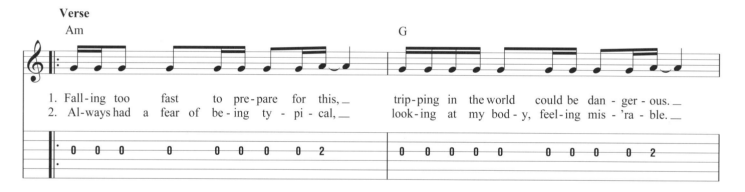

Ev-'ry-bod-y cir-cl-ing, it's vul-tur-ous, ___ neg-a-tive, ___ nep-o-tist. ___
Al-ways hang-ing on to the vis-u-al, ___ I want to be ___ in-vis-i-ble. ___

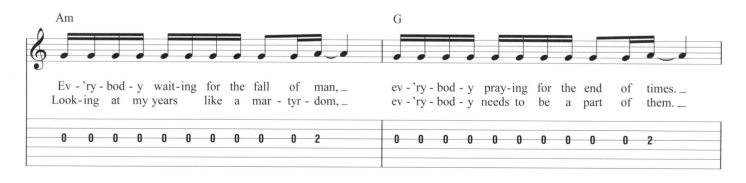

Ev-'ry-bod-y wait-ing for the fall of man, ___ ev-'ry-bod-y pray-ing for the end of times. ___
Look-ing at my years like a mar-tyr-dom, ___ ev-'ry-bod-y needs to be a part of them. ___

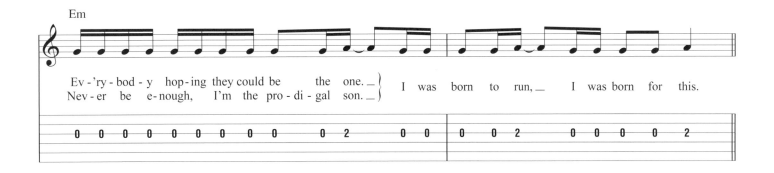

Ev-'ry-bod-y hop-ing they could be the one. __
Nev-er be e-nough, I'm the pro-di-gal son. __
I was born to run, __ I was born for this.

Pre-Chorus

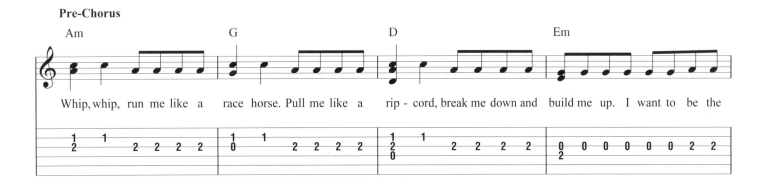

Whip, whip, run me like a race horse. Pull me like a rip-cord, break me down and build me up. I want to be the

slip, slip, word up-on your lip, lip. Let-ter that you rip, rip. Break me down and build me up. What-ev-er it takes, __

𝄋 **Chorus**

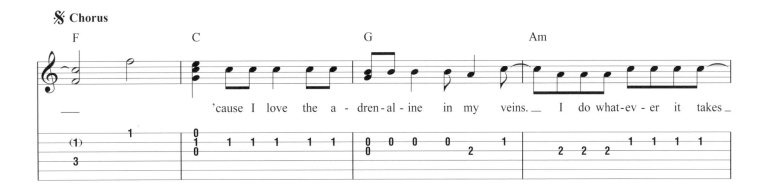

__ 'cause I love the a-dren-al-ine in my veins. __ I do what-ev-er it takes __

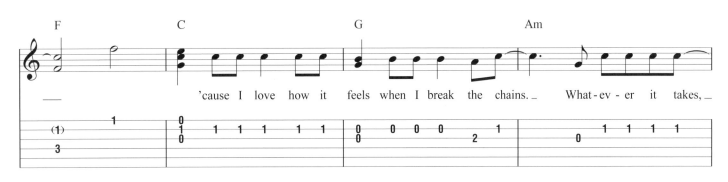

__ 'cause I love how it feels when I break the chains. __ What-ev-er it takes, __

you take me to the top. I'm read-y for what-ev-er it takes _

3rd time, To Coda ⊕

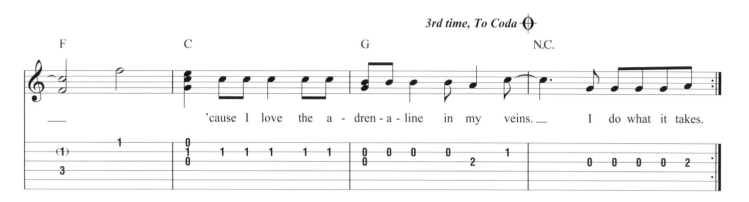

'cause I love the a - dren - a - line in my veins. _ I do what it takes.

Verse

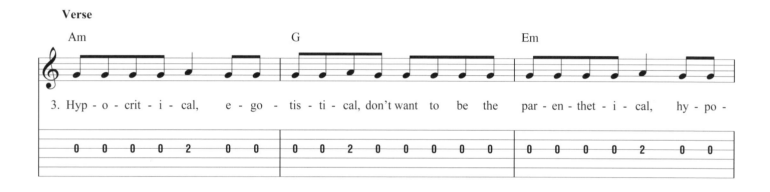

3. Hyp - o - crit - i - cal, e - go - tis - ti - cal, don't want to be the par - en - thet - i - cal, hy - po -

thet - i - cal. Work-ing on to some-thing that I'm proud of, out of the box, _ an e - pox -

- y to the world and the vi - sion we've lost. _ I'm an a - pos - tro - phe, I'm just a

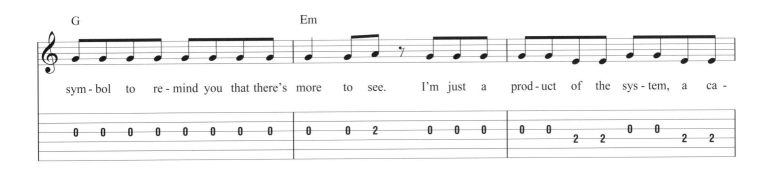

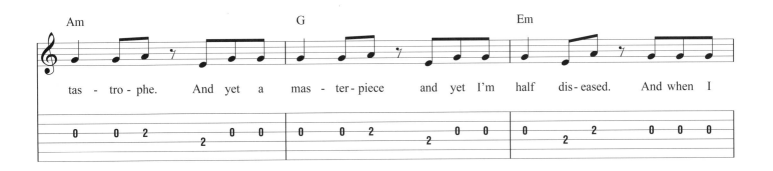

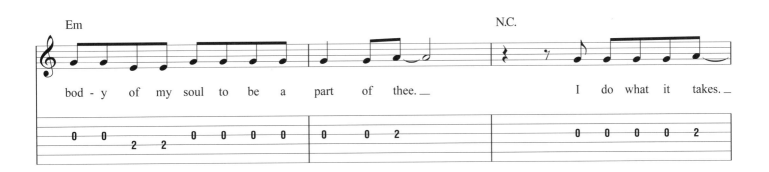

D.S. al Coda   Coda

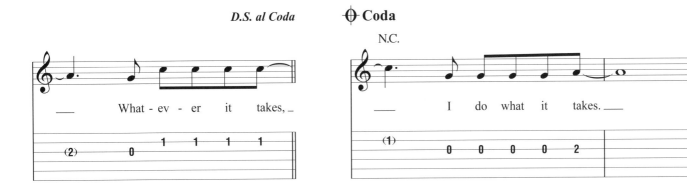

You Are the Reason

Words and Music by Calum Scott, Corey Sanders and Jonathan Maguire

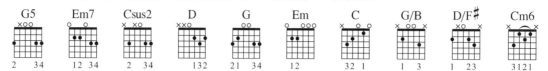

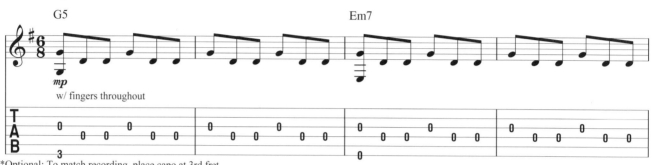

*Capo III

Strum Pattern: 8
Pick Pattern: 8

Intro
Slow, in 2

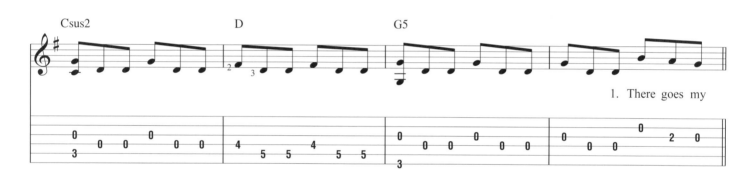

w/ fingers throughout

*Optional: To match recording, place capo at 3rd fret.

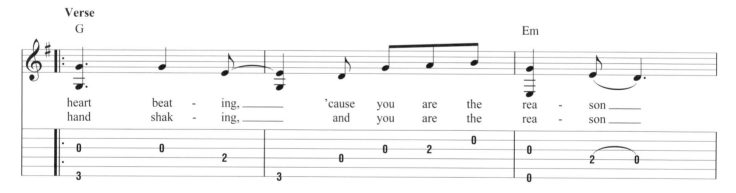

1. There goes my

Verse

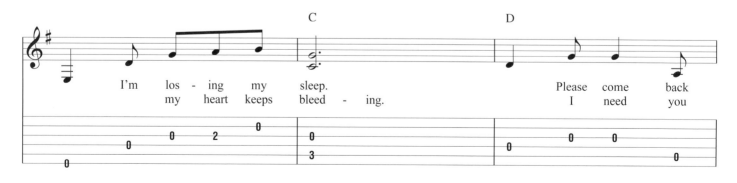

heart   beat - ing, _____   'cause you   are   the   rea - son _____
hand   shak - ing, _____   and you   are   the   rea - son _____

I'm   los - ing   my   sleep.   Please   come   back
my   heart   keeps   bleed - ing.   I   need   you

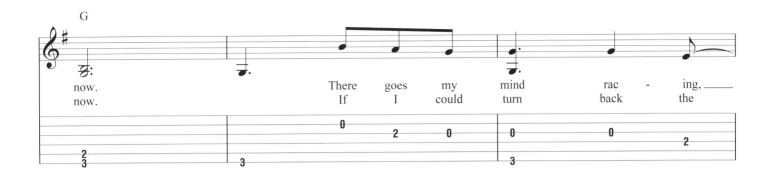

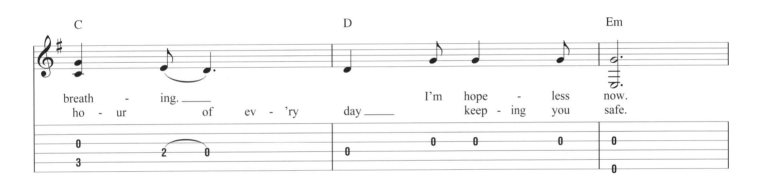

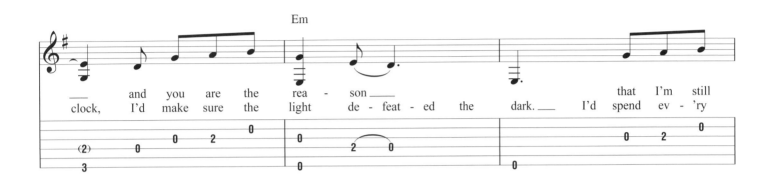

Chorus

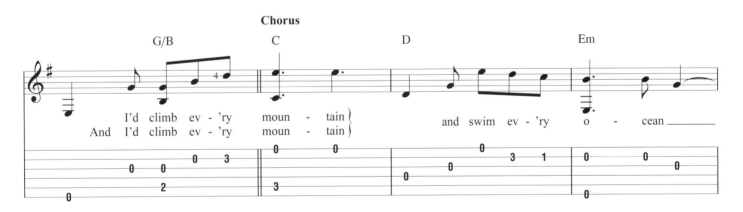

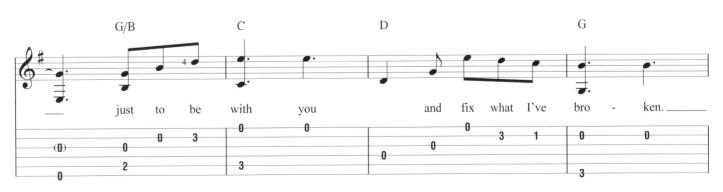

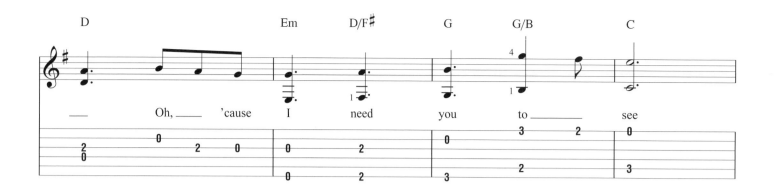

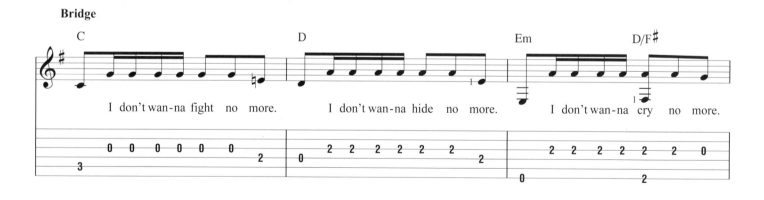

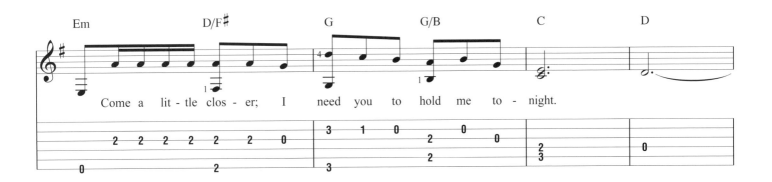

Come a lit - tle clos - er; I need you to hold me to - night.

Outro-Chorus

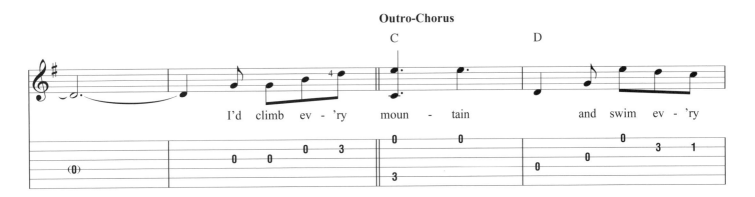

I'd climb ev - 'ry moun - tain and swim ev - 'ry

o - cean just to be with you and fix what I've

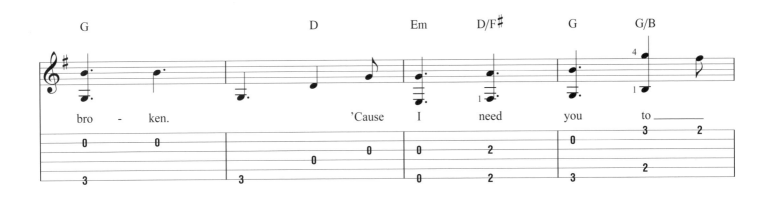

bro - ken. 'Cause I need you to

see that you are the rea - son.

Tequila

Words and Music by Dan Smyers, Jordan Reynolds and Nicolle Galyon

*Capo IV

Strum Pattern: 6
Pick Pattern: 2

Intro
Moderately slow, in 2

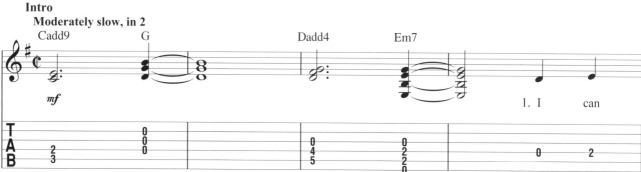

*Optional: To match recording, place capo at 4th fret.

Verse

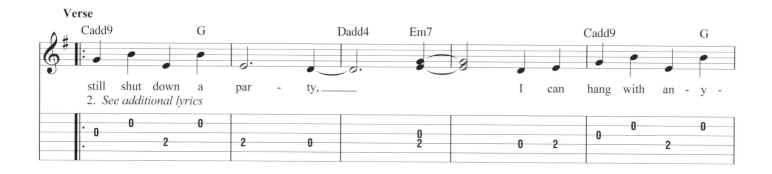

still shut down a par - ty, _____ I can hang with an - y -
2. *See additional lyrics*

bod - y. _____ I can drink whis - key _____ and red _____ wine, cham-

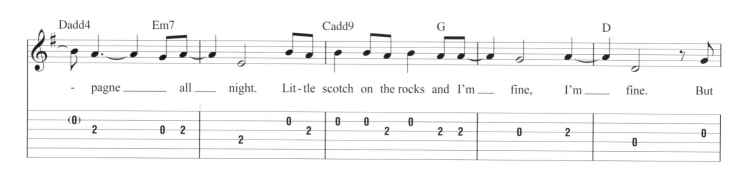

- pagne _____ all _____ night. Lit - tle scotch on the rocks and I'm _____ fine, I'm _____ fine. But

Additional Lyrics

2. I can kiss somebody brand-new
And not even think about you.
I can show up to the same bar,
Hear the same songs in my car.
Baby, your mem'ry, it only hits me this hard
When I taste tequila…